I0513368

Dear Chris,

You will find enclosed just one example of the anticipated liability of Credit Card Companies who have perpetuated the financial scandal of our generation, namely; Collateralised Credit Exploitation (CCE) which is characterized as unwarranted entrapment which interminably indentures some of their best clients to long term financial slavery. This example serves to represent the 'Billions which will be repaid to Millions' due to Credit Card Companies cynically and persistently exploiting vulnerable customers from whom they are reputed to gain 50% of their corporate profits. CCE has been established as carrying NO 'Value at Risk', NO Probability of Risk with an amount at risk of NIL but most tellingly where they have already been *repaid* their capital at up to 11x the original sum they still charge unwarranted, usurious and extortionate interest rates, fees and charges on their most vulnerable customers. Treating their BEST customers as 'can be abused junk accounts' when they are proven AAA+ is clearly & demonstrably 'fraudulently counterfactual'. The 'corporately designed' failure of Credit Card Companies to make a simple and generally accepted risk weighted calculation on CCE client credit cards (up to 1,151% positive return has been estimated) have been universally condemned as being unreasonable & exploitative.

How MUCH is ENOUGH!!!

Collateralised Credit Exploitation as practised on AAA None Defaulting accounts is in effect an Annuity in Perpetuity and is demonstrably Exploitative by Design -Extortionate by Intent - Fraudulent by Nature.

Our political & regulatory & financial establishment has demonstrated endogenously heterodoxical behaviour in their collective incapacity to respect the UK Citizen by ignoring the fact of and the damage caused by Collateralised Credit Exploitation.

Exploitative By Design - Extortionate By Intent - Fraudulent By Nature

Billions will be repaid to Millions' estimated cost to Credit Card Companies of Collateralised Credit Exploitation is conservatively put at between £50-75 Billion. Collateralised Credit Exploitation by Credit Card Companies is the cynical long term exploitation of vulnerable customers where there is no risk and no probability of risk to Credit Card Companies who perpetuate the practice.

One Example amongst millions, follows;

>**New Day Opus** £ 110,000 gross on 10,000 @ 48.1% over 20 years*
>**New Day Marbles** £ 84,000 gross on 9,000 @ 39.9% over 20 years*
>**Capital One** £ 27,000 gross on 2.500 @ 31.1% over 20 years*
>**MBNA** £ 76,000 gross on 8,000 @ 30.0% over 20 years*,
>£ 46,000 gross on 5.000 @ 30.0% over 20 years*,
>£ 12,000 gross on 3,000 @ 30.0% over 20 years*
>**BarclayCard** £ 43,000 gross on 5.500 @ 26.5% over 20 years*
>£ 20,000 gross on 3,000 @ 26.5% over 20 years*
>**RBS** £ 85,000 gross on 14,000 @ 16.9% over 20 years*

£ **503**,000 to be **repaid** on £ **54**,000

*Each Credit Card to confirm exact extortion period & exploitative interest rate.

All amounts above are **PLUS** interest, charges, fees, fines & compensation conservatively creating a £**754.500** Collateralised Credit Exploitation Liability on 1) on six credit card companies (above) on 2) nine numbered cards over 20 exemplary years. Base Rate 0.25% to 0.50%. Credit Card Companies have been allowed to insidiously develop over time a purposefully distorted Credit Risk Analysis Model which effectively penalizes their best customers & imbalances the relationship between avaricious providers & vulnerable users of credit instruments. Collateralized Credit Exploitation clearly demonstrates that the 'Value at Risk' nexus does NOT exist for the Credit Card Company & that they are imposing unreasonable and extortionate charges onto the consumer. Rather than 'know' they are 'ignoring the rights & abasing the needs' of their customers.

Credit Card Companies have been allowed to insidiously develop over time a purposefully distorted Credit Risk Analysis Model which effectively penalizes their best customers and imbalances the relationship between avaricious providers & vulnerable users of credit instruments.

'Collateralized Credit Exploitation or CCE (Cynical Long Term Revolver Entrapment) is the scourge of our generation perpetrated with impunity by Credit Card Companies'

We have recently published our TimeOutCreditCards Exploitation Index (CCE Scandal Scenario) as follows: No.1 = No Counter Party Risk, No. 2 = Annuity in Perpetuity, No.3 = AAA None Defaulting, No.4 = PFI - PPI of which CCE is the greatest injustice, No.5 = Unregulated Financial Misconduct, No.6 = Unjustified Financial Exploitation, No.7 = Persistent Imperious Exploitation, No.8 = Abuse of any generally acceptable prudential regime, No 9 = Devoid of commonly accepted rationality or merit No. 10 = Fails any and every measure of financial risk based ethical behavior.

Interested parties across the world have now been invited to join the Movement @TimeOutCreditCards #PutAnEndToFinancialSlavery.

Several connected publications and keynote presentations are available T.V. Radio & Social, Business & Trade Media notified. Legacy Societal Adverse Impacts & Abusive Effects - Just ONE Example

Principal (with 9 cards from 6 companies MBNA, Capital One, RBS, BarclayCard, New Day Opus & Marbles) £ 54,000 Amount Repaid (estimated over 20 years) £ 503.000. 9 x Credit Cards from 6 Credit Card Companies interest up to 48.1% (base rate 0.25% to 0.50%). Risk Weighted Asset - up to 1,151% positive return. After almost 20 years as an impeccable payer our borrower asked politely over a period of time (2013 - 2018) 9 Credit Card companies to reduce their high rates of up to 48%+ so that they could be paid off, ALL REFUSED !!!

Repayment of those 9 cards on a principal amount of £ 54,000will have up to 20 years incur estimated gross payments of £ 503,000 (each credit card company has been asked to provide accurate payment amounts or engage in constructive discussion with the payee but each has effectively declined to do so) No financial organization has the right to impose a combination of excessive and unwarranted interest + charges + punitive fees on nominal amounts that cannot be paid back within an individual's lifetime by creating sustained (Collateralized Credit Exploitation) CCEs at rates which are not supported by any rational, reasonable, ethical measure or by any accepted financial risk ratios or prudential regime.

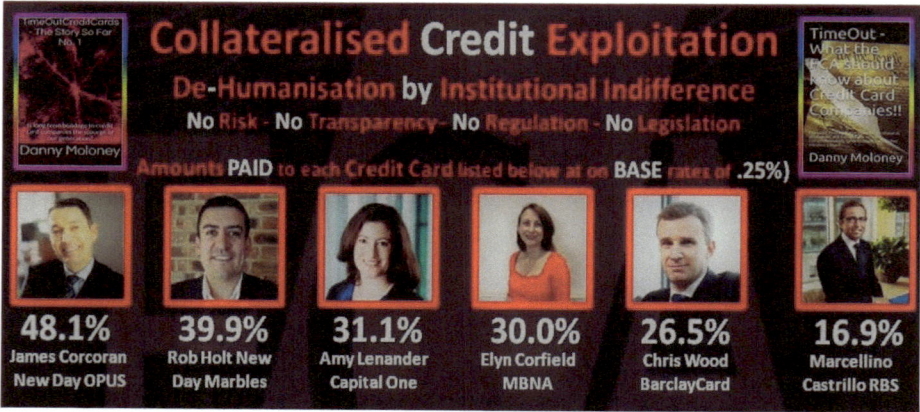

De Humanization by Institutional Indifference

Principal - £54,000
Estimated Amount Repaid** - £503,000
Over Length of Time* - 0 to 20 years
Credit Card Interest – up to 48.1%
Bank of England Base Rate – 0.25 % to 0.50%

Amount to be repaid by the Credit Card Companies
Principal + OverPayment + Interest + Charges + Compensation =
£ 503.000*** (estimate)

Status - Creditor of each credit card named above

CCE Value at Risk (VaR) Time Frame - Lifetime, Amount at Risk - NIL, Probability of Risk - NIL, Collateralized Credit Exploitation is cynical long term entrapment & unconscionable financial slavery where there is No Risk - No Transparency - No Regulation - No Legislation.

*Each Credit Card Company have to date withheld the necessary information to make an accurate calculation of total payments made ** Each Credit Card Company can provide a more detailed breakdown. *** Projection. Account Number for 9 x cards ending (available)

How MUCH is ENOUGH!!!

Collateralised Credit Exploitation is practiced on AAA None Defaulting accounts & is in effect an Annuity in Perpetuity and is demonstrably Exploitative by Design -Extortionate by Intent - Fraudulent by Nature.

Our political & regulatory & financial establishment has demonstrated endogenously heterodoxical behaviour in their collective incapacity to respect the UK Citizen by ignoring the fact of and the damage caused by Collateralised Credit Exploitation.

Danny Moloney, MBA, MSc, MA, MAPCE, MACT (DBA IP).
Greater Eccles, Manchester, United Kingdom.
Sunday 8th July 2018

Find Out More On: @TimeOutCCards and/or @DisCreditCards *and/or* TimeOutCreditCards – The Story So Far - No.1 https://www.amazon.co.uk/dp/B01N393PDI *and/or*
What The FCA Should Know About Credit Cards https://www.amazon.co.uk/dp/B073Z1YVNT and/or Chronolog 'Talk To Us, Prime Minister' https://www.amazon.co.uk/dp/B07FC2TJHY
and/or Chronolog 'Financial Slavery by Credit Card Companies '
https://www.amazon.co.uk/dp/B07FM664XV
and/or Genesis 'Billions will be REPAID to Millions – TimeOutCreditCards – Chris Wood

Breaking Free of the Shackles of Financial Slavery

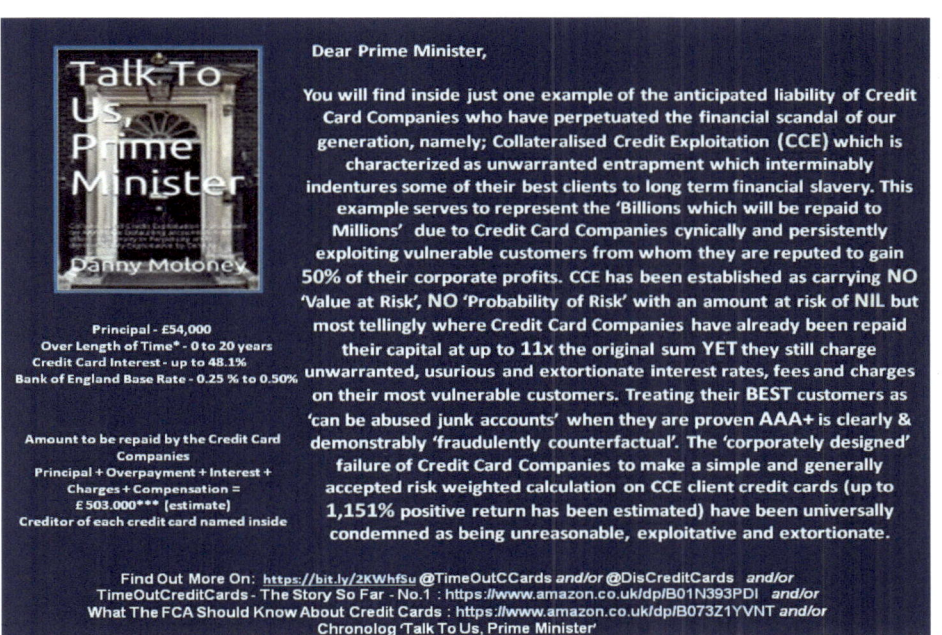

Talk to us, Prime Minister

Letter One 15th April 2018 – Chris Wood
Greater Eccles, Manchester, M30 7AZ

Telephone - + 161 789 8787   e-mail sales@globalmehpte.com

Chris Wood
BarclayCard Commercial
P. O. Box 4000
Saffron Road
Wigston
LE18 9EN   Sunday 15th April 2018

Dear Chris,
                                                          Barclaycard No. ending 6231
                                                          Your Ref: 547676 0028852716
                                    BarclayCard Commercial **9** - 1997 - 2007 - 2017 - 2027

We write to you now concerning Collateralized Credit Exploitation (or with direct reference to the Financial Conduct Authority's recently published study on 'Persistent Debt') now being referred to as 'Persistent Exploitation' by Credit Card Companies.

We attach overleaf a courtesy copy of a letter sent to Mrs. Theresa May in the hope that she may be able to help to bring such Unregulated Credit Card Company Behavior to a swift equitable denouement and that you may make a contribution to that long overdue debate on behalf of BarclayCard

Yours Sincerely,

Danny Moloney, MBA.

Overleaf are our interim calculations of gross payments made to BarclayCard 1

Letter One 15th April 2018 - Theresa May

Greater Eccles, Manchester, M30 7AZ, U.K.

Telephone: 0161 789 8787   Email: timeoutcreditcards@globalmehpte.com

Mrs. Theresa May,   Theresa May - 1
10 Downing Street,
Westminster
London,
SW 1A 2AA   April 15th 2018

'The financialisation of our economy has rendered political institutions virtually powerless to represent the interests of UK consumers'.

Dear Mrs. May,

I write on this occasion to represent millions of U.K. citizens, who daily labor under the insidious burden of Collateralised Credit Exploitation (a perversely distorted and financially reprehensible loan to payment ratio) perpetrated by the named Credit Card Companies and tacitly supported by the Government Bodies, Authorities & Associations, also named below.

Andrew Bailey at the FCA has attempted to deal with the scandal by addressing 'Persistent Debt' but the real issue is 'Persistent Exploitation' by unregulated Credit Card Companies.

Credit Card Companies - The Perpetrators

MBNA - Elyn Corfield , OPUS - James Corcoran, MARBLES - Rob Holt, Royal Bank of Scotland - Marcellino Castrillo, Capital One - Amy Lenander, Barclaycard - Chris Wood

Government Bodies & Authorities & Associations - The Regulators

Financial Ombudsman - Caroline Wayman, Prudential Regulation Authority - Mark Carney, Competition & Markets Authority - Andrea Coscelli, Payment Systems Regulator - Hannah Nixon, Philip Hammond - Chancellor of the Exchequer, Andrew Bailey - Financial Conduct Authority, UK Cards Association - Graham Peacop, Finance & Leasing Association - Richard Jones, British Bankers Association - Eric Leenders, Lending & Standards - Board Dave Pickering & Money Advice Service - Charles Counsell.

I would like you to invite those named above to meet with you and I at 10 Downing Street, the seat of our executive government to answer the questions from myself, 1) Why the Credit Card Companies & the Government Bodies & Authorities have behaved like this and effectively allowed this scandal to persist & from you; 2) What are they going to do about it?

Thanks for your support in resolving this demonstrable and injurious evil within our society.

Danny Moloney
Greater Eccles, Manchester, United Kingdom

Letter Two 14th May 2018 – Chris Wood

Greater Eccles, Manchester, M30 7AZ

Telephone - 0161 789 8787 e-mail info@globalmehpte.com

Chris Wood
BarclayCard Commercial
P. O. Box 4000
Saffron Road
Wigston
LE18 9EN

Barclaycard Nos. ending 6231/6003
Your Ref: 547676 0028852716
BarclayCard Commercial **10** - 1997 - 2007 - 2017 - 2027

Dear Chris, Monday 14th May 2018

'**Collateralized Credit Exploitation or CCE** (Cynical Long Term Revolver Entrapment)
is the scourge of our generation perpetrated with impunity by Credit Card Companies'

Further to our letter to you of 15/4/18, to which we await your reply.

We have recently published our **TimeOutCreditCards Exploitation Index** (CCE Scandal Scenario) as follows: **No.**1 = No Counter Party Risk, **No.** 2 = Annuity in Perpetuity, **No.**3 = AAA None Defaulting, **No.**4 = PFI - PPI of which CCE is the greatest injustice, **No.**5 = Unregulated Financial Misconduct, **No.**6 = Unjustified Financial Exploitation, **No.**7 = Persistent Impunious Exploitation, **No.**8 = Abuse of any generally acceptable prudential regime, **No** 9 = Devoid of commonly accepted rationality or merit **No. 10** = Fails any and every measure of financial risk based ethical behavior.

Interested parties across the world have now been invited to join the Movement @TimeOutCreditCards #PutAnEndToFinancialSlavery. Several connected publications and keynote presentations are available T.V. Radio & Social, Business & Trade Media notified.

Thank you for your support in resolving this demonstrable, injurious, flagrant and persistent financial slavery within our society.

Danny Moloney, Restitutional Activist, Greater Eccles, Manchester, United Kingdom

Legacy Societal Adverse Impacts & Abusive Effects - Just ONE Example

Principal (with 9 cards from 6 companies MBNA, Capital One, RBS, BarclayCard, New Day Opus & Marbles) **£ 60.799** Amount Repaid (estimated over 20 years) **£ 472.001** Amount which will be Repaid (estimated over 30 years) **£ 699.933.**
9 x Credit Cards from 6 Credit Card Companies interest up to 48.1% (base rate 0.25% to 0.50%). Risk Weighted Asset - up to **1,151%** positive return. After almost 20 years as an impeccable payer our borrower asked politely over a period of time (2013 - 2017) 9 Credit Card companies to reduce their high rates of up to 48%+ so that they could be paid off, **ALL REFUSED !!!**

Repayment of those 9 cards on a principal amount of £ 60,799 will have up to 20 years incur estimated gross payments of £ 472,001 and over 30 years will incur estimated gross payments of £ 699,933 (each credit card company has been asked to provide accurate payment amounts or engage in constructive discussion with the payee but each has effectively declined to do so) No financial organization has the right to impose a combination of excessive and unwarranted interest + charges + punitive fees on nominal amounts that cannot be paid back within an individual's lifetime by creating sustained (Collateralized Credit Exploitation)
CCEs at rates which are not supported by any rational, reasonable, ethical measure or by any accepted financial risk ratios or prudential regime.

Principal - **£60,799**   Estimated Amount Repaid** - **£472,001**   Over Length of Time* - **0 to 20 years**

Credit Card Interest – up to **48.1%**   Bank of England Base Rate – 0.25 % to **0.50%**

Amount to be repaid by the Credit Card Companies
Principal + OverPayment + Interest + Charges + Compensation = £ 350,403.00***
(estimate)

Status - Creditor of each credit card named above

*Each Credit Card Company have to date withheld the necessary information to make an accurate calculation of total payments made ** Each Credit Card Company can provide a more detailed breakdown. *** Projection. Account for 9 x cards ending (available)

Letter Three 20th June 2018 – Chris Wood

Greater Eccles, Manchester, M30 7AZ

Telephone - + 44 161 789 8787   e-mail timeoutcreditcards@globalmehpte.com

Chris Wood   Chris - 3
BarclayCard Commercial
P. O. Box 4000   Barclaycard Nos. ending 6231/6003
Saffron Road   Your Ref: 547676 0028852716
Wigston   BarclayCard Personal & Commercial 11 - 1997 - 2007 - 2017 - 2027
LE18 9EN   Wednesday 20th June 2018

Billions will be repaid to Millions of UK Consumers

Dear Chris,

Further to our letters to you of 15/4/18 & 14/5/18, to which we await your reply.

We look forward to the Collateralized Credit Exploitation Summit to be held at Downing Street, which will be followed by presentations across the country entitled 'Ending Financial Slavery to Credit Card Companies'.

Thank you for your support in resolving this demonstrable, injurious, flagrant and persistent financial evil within our society.

Danny Moloney
Restitutional Activist
Greater Eccles, Manchester, United Kingdom

Legacy Societal Adverse Impacts & Abusive Effects - Just ONE Example

We have recently published our **TimeOutCreditCards Exploitation Index** (CCE Scandal Scenario) as follows: **No.1** = No Counter Party Risk, **No. 2** = Annuity in Perpetuity, **No.3** = AAA None Defaulting, **No.4** = PFI - PPI of which CCE is the greatest injustice, **No.5** = Unregulated Financial Misconduct, **No.6** = Unjustified Financial Exploitation, **No.7** = Persistent Impunious Exploitation, **No.8** = Abuse of any generally acceptable prudential regime, **No 9** = Devoid of commonly accepted rationality or merit **No. 10** = Fails any and every measure of financial risk based ethical behavior.

Principal (with 9 cards from 6 companies MBNA, Capital One, RBS, BarclayCard, New Day Opus & Marbles)) **£ 60.799** Amount Repaid (estimated over 20 years) **£ 472.001** Amount which will be Repaid (estimated over 30 years) **£ 699.933.**
9 x Credit Cards from 6 Credit Card Companies interest up to 48.1% (base rate 0.25% to 0.50%) Risk Weighted Asset - up to **1,151%** positive return. After almost 20 years as an impeccable payer our borrower asked politely over a period of time (2013 - 2017) 9 Credit Card companies to reduce their high rates of up to 48%+ so that they could be paid off, **ALL REFUSED !!!**

Repayment of those 9 cards on a principal amount of £ 60,799 will have up to 20 years incur estimated gross payments of £ 472,001 and over 30 years will incur estimated gross payments of £ 699,933 (each credit card company has been asked to provide accurate payment amounts or engage in constructive discussion with the payee but each has effectively declined to do so) No financial organization has the right to impose a combination of excessive and unwarranted interest + charges + punitive fees on nominal amounts that cannot be paid back within an individual's lifetime by creating sustained (Collateralized Credit Exploitation)
CCEs at rates which are not supported by any rational, reasonable, ethical measure or by any accepted financial risk ratios or prudential regime.

Principal - **£60,799**
Estimated Amount Repaid** - **£472,001**
Over Length of Time* - **0** to **20 years**
Credit Card Interest – up to **48.1%**

Bank of England Base Rate – 0.25 % to **0.50%**

Amount to be repaid by the Credit Card Companies
Principal + OverPayment + Interest + Charges + Compensation = £ 350,403.00***
(estimate)

Status - Creditor of each credit card named above.

*Each Credit Card Company have to date withheld the necessary information to make an accurate calculation of total payments made ** Each Credit Card Company can provide a more detailed breakdown. *** Projection. Account for 9 x cards ending (available)

Letter Four 9th July 2018 – Chris Wood
Greater Eccles, Manchester, M30 7AZ
Telephone - + 44 161 789 8787   e-mail timeoutcreditcards@globalmehpte.com

Chris Wood   Chris - 4
BarclayCard Commercial
P. O. Box 4000   Barclaycard Nos. ending 6231/6003
Saffron Road   Your Ref: 547676 0028852716
Wigston   BarclayCard Personal & Commercial 12 - 1997 - 2007 - 2017 - 2027
LE18 9EN   Monday 9th July 2018

Dear Chris,

You will find overleaf just one example of the anticipated liability of Credit Card Companies who have perpetuated the financial scandal of our generation, namely; Collateralized Credit Exploitation (CCE) which is characterized as unwarranted entrapment which interminably indentures some of their best clients to long term financial slavery. This example serves to represent the 'Billions which will be repaid to Millions' due to Credit Card Companies cynically and persistently exploiting vulnerable customers from whom they are reputed to gain 50% of their corporate profits. CCE has been established as carrying **NO** 'Value at Risk', **NO** 'Probability of Risk' with an amount at risk of **NIL** but most tellingly where they have already been *repaid* their capital at up to **11x** the original sum they still charge unwarranted, usurious and extortionate interest rates, fees and charges on their most vulnerable customers. Treating their BEST customers as 'can be abused junk accounts' when they are proven AAA+ is clearly & demonstrably 'fraudulently counterfactual'. The 'corporately designed' failure of Credit Card Companies to make a simple and generally accepted risk weighted calculation on CCE client credit cards (up to 1,151% positive return has been estimated) have been universally condemned as being unreasonable & exploitative.

How MUCH is ENOUGH!!!

Collateralised Credit Exploitation is practiced on AAA None Defaulting accounts & is in effect an Annuity in Perpetuity and is demonstrably Exploitative by Design -Extortionate by Intent - Fraudulent by Nature.

Our political & regulatory & financial establishment has demonstrated endogenously heterodoxical behavior in their collective incapacity to respect the UK Citizen by ignoring the fact of and the damage caused by Collateralised Credit Exploitation.

Danny Moloney,
MBA, MSc, MA, MAPCE, MACT (DBA IP).
Greater Eccles, Manchester, United Kingdom.
Sunday 8th July 2018

Exploitative By Design - Extortionate By Intent - Fraudulent By Nature

Billions will be repaid to Millions' estimated cost to Credit Card Companies of Collateralised Credit Exploitation is conservatively put at between £50-75 Billion. Collateralised Credit Exploitation by Credit Card Companies is the cynical long term exploitation of vulnerable customers where there is no risk and no probability of risk to Credit Card Companies who perpetuate the practice.

One Example amongst millions, follows;

*Each Credit Card to confirm exact extortion period & exploitative interest rate.

New Day Opus £ 110,000 gross on 10,000 @ 48.1% over 20 years*

New Day Marbles £ 84,000 gross on 9,000 @ 39.9% over 20 years*

Capital One £ 27,000 gross on 2.500 @ 31.1% over 20 years*

MBNA £ 76,000 gross on 8,000 @ 30.0% over 20 years*,

£ 46,000 gross on 5.000 @ 30.0% over 20 years*,

£ 12,000 gross on 3,000 @ 30.0% over 20 years*

BarclayCard £ 43,000 gross on 5.500 @ 26.5% over 20 years*

£ 20,000 gross on 3,000 @ 26.5% over 20 years*

RBS £ 85,000 gross on 14,000 @ 16.9% over 20 years*

£ **503,000** to be repaid on **£ 54,000**

All amounts above are **PLUS** interest, charges, fees, fines & compensation conservatively creating a £**754.500** Collateralized Credit Exploitation Liability on 1) on six credit card companies (above) on 2) nine numbered cards over 20 exemplary years. Base Rate 0.25% to 0.50%. Credit Card Companies have been allowed to insidiously develop over time a purposefully distorted Credit Risk Analysis Model which effectively penalizes their best customers & imbalances the relationship between avaricious providers & vulnerable users of credit instruments. Collateralized Credit Exploitation clearly demonstrates that the 'Value at Risk' nexus does NOT exist for the Credit Card Company & that they are imposing unreasonable and extortionate charges onto the consumer. Rather than 'know' they are 'ignoring the rights & abasing the needs' of their customers. Credit Card Companies have been allowed to insidiously develop over time a purposefully distorted Credit Risk Analysis Model which effectively penalizes their best customers and imbalances the relationship between avaricious providers & vulnerable users of credit instruments.

Find Out More On: @TimeOutCCards and/or @DisCreditCards *and/or* TimeOutCreditCards – The Story So Far - No.1 https://www.amazon.co.uk/dp/B01N393PDI *and/or*
What The FCA Should Know About Credit Cards https://www.amazon.co.uk/dp/B073Z1YVNT
and/or Chronolog 'Talk To Us, Prime Minister' https://www.amazon.co.uk/dp/B07FC2TJHY
and/or Chronolog 'Financial Slavery by Credit Card Companies '
https://www.amazon.co.uk/dp/B07FM664XV
and/or Genesis 'Billions will be REPAID to Millions – TimeOutCreditCards – Chris Wood

TimeOutCreditCards

Collateralised Credit Exploitation

New Day Opus - New Day Marbles - Capital One - MBNA - Barclaycard - RBS

Your MOST profitable customers have rights too for Justice and Respect.

It is no surprise that James Corcoran of New Day Opus, Rob Holt of New Day Marbles, Amy Lenander of Capital One, Elyn Corfield of MBNA, Chris Wood of BarclayCard & Marcellino Castrillo of Royal Bank of Scotland, have not responded to letters sent to each one of them personally and provided a personalized response by way of explanation as to their collective behavior in perpetrating the financial scandal of our generation - Collateralized Credit Exploitation.

TimeOutCreditCards Collateralised Credit Exploitation has impaired the inherent right of individual or collective customers for equitable financial management.

If Politicians - Regulators - Credit Card Companies fail to support the best interests of a member of the public; they are entitled to take the measures necessary to maintain respect and bring an end to exploitation exemplified by TimeOutCreditCards Collateralised Credit Exploitation, which has been proven to be Credit Exploitation & Financial Slavery.

Customers are equally entitled to a level of support which should be designed and is subsequently conducted in accordance with recognized best practice and ethical standards.

Customers have the right to expect Politicians - Regulators to use commonly accepted standards commonly assess, confirm and improve their governance and financial management policies and practice and be accountable to their customers for their malpractice.

Politicians - Regulators have implicit responsibility to protect and safeguard customers from extortion by unregulated Credit Card Companies.

Collateralised Credit Exploitation is a clear case of financial exploitation, it was the very scenario that the Legislatory & Regulatory framework has been designed to confront, challenge, manage & control in the interests of consumers.

'No financial organization has the right to make excessive interest & charges on nominal amounts that cannot be paid back within an individual's lifetime by creating (Collateralised Credit Exploitation) CCEs'

""'It should be easier for consumers to challenge unfair agreements and that the definition of 'extortionate' should be widened to cover unfair practices both at the time of entering the credit agreement as well as any subsequent events that may have led to unfairness"".

Detailed information has been provided to the 6 x Credit Card Companies
(NINE cards in total)

(MBNA Elyn Corfield - Capital One Amy Lenander - New Day Marbles Rob Holt - BarclayCard Chris Wood - RBS Marcellino Castrillo - New Day Opus - James Corcoran) who are known and are evidenced to practice Collateralised Credit Exploitation (CCE)

The Financial Conduct Authority Andrew Bailey - The Financial Ombudsman Caroline Wayman - The UK Cards Association Graham Peacop - The Prudential Regulation Authority Mark Carney - The Finance & Leasing Association Richard Jones - The British Bankers Association Eric Leenders - The Competition & Markets Authority Andrea Coscelli - The UK Parliament Phillip Hammond - The Lending & Standards Board Dave Pickering - The Payment Systems Regulator Hannah Nixon - The Money Advice Service Charles Counsell have been made fully aware of the practice of Collateralised Credit Exploitation (CCE).

EVERY Member of Parliament has victims of Collateralised Credit Exploitation in his or her constituency; suffering under the pain of unreasonable, unwarranted and unjustified behavior by Credit Card Companies.

British consumers have been slavishly providing extortionate, unjustified & unwarranted profits for Credit Card Companies for generations under the indefensibly false guise of 'long revolver credit' and are now holding them to account for their unwarranted financial profligacy of people's lives, their relationships, their income, their marriages & their life chances. Collateralised Credit Exploitation is entrapment & financial slavery

'Billions will be repaid to Millions' initial estimate of the cost to Credit Card Companies of Collateralised Credit Exploitation is conservatively put at between £50 - 75 Billion.

Exploitative By Design - Extortionate By Intent - Fraudulent By Nature

Never in the annals of financial history has so much been taken from so many by so few.

TimeOutCreditCards Collateralised Credit Exploitation: Never in the Annals of Financial History

Collateralised Credit Exploitation
De-Humanisation by Institutional Indifference
No Risk - No Transparency - No Regulation - No Legislation

Treating their BEST customers as 'can be abused junk accounts' when they are proven AAA+ is clearly & demonstrably 'fraudulently counterfactual' !!!

- Amy Lenander — Capital One — 31.1%
- James Corcoran — New Day OPUS — 48.1%
- Chris Wood — BarclayCard — 26.5%
- Marcellino Castrillo RBS — 16.9%
- Elyn Corfield — MBNA — 30.0%
- Rob Holt New Day Marbles — 39.9%

- John McDonnell — MP
- Andrew Bailey — FCA
- Theresa May — MP
- REDlined — Ending Financial Slavery
- Jeremy Corbyn — MP
- Mark Carney — BoE
- Phil Hammond — MP

TimeOutCreditCards Collateralised Credit Exploitation: Treating AAA+ Customers as Junk Accounts

---

TimeOutCreditCards

Collateralised Credit Exploitation is
#LongTermEntrapment, #ImmoralHazard,
#FinancialSlavery, #Extortion,
#NoCounterPartyRisk, #NoCreditRisk,
#AnnuityInPerpetuity, #AAANoneDefaulting,
#UnregulatedFinancialMisConDuct,
#UnjustifiedFinancialExploitation,
#MisAppropriatedEquity #DevoidOfMerit,
#NoFinancialRisk, #UnEthical, #Scandal
#PersistentImpuniousExploitation,
YET it is acceptable to Credit Card Companies, Financial Regulators and Politicians of all parties.

- Amy Lenander — Capital One — 31.1%
- James Corcoran — New Day - OPUS — 48.1%
- Chris Wood — BarclayCard — 26.5%
- Marcellino Castrillo - RBS — 16.9%
- Elyn Corfield — MBNA — 30.0%
- Rob Holt - New Day - Marbles — 39.9%

- John McDonald — MP
- Andrew Bailey — FCA
- Theresa May — MP
- Parliamentarians
- Jeremy Corbyn — MP
- Mark Carney — BoE
- Phil Hammond — MP

REDlined - Ending Financial Slavery

TimeOutCreditCards Collateralised Credit Exploitation: REDlined Ending Financial Slavery

TimeOutCreditCards Collateralised Credit Exploitation: NO Risk BUT exploitative Rewards!!!

TimeOutCreditCards Collateralised Credit Exploitation: Cynical Use of Long Term Entrapment

TimeOutCreditCards Collateralised Credit Exploitation: How can Legislators & Regulators allow this to happen?

TimeOutCreditCards Collateralised Credit Exploitation: It is NO surprise that there is NO response

TimeOutCreditCards Collateralised Credit Exploitation: Billions will be REPAID to millions

TimeOutCreditCards Collateralised Credit Exploitation: Talk to us, Prime Minister

TimeOutCreditCards Collateralised Credit Exploitation: Endogenously Heterodoxical

TimeOutCreditCards Collateralised Credit Exploitation: Should PAY, Won't PAY!!!

TimeOutCreditCards Collateralised Credit Exploitation: he Who Accepts Evil

TimeOutCreditCards Collateralised Credit Exploitation: CCE Value AT Risk?

TimeOutCreditCards Extortion Index

9 x Credit Cards from 6 Credit Card Companies Interest up to 48.1% (Bank Base Rate 0.25 to 0.50%)
Client Risk Weighted Asset - up to 1,151% positive return with NO Counter Party Risk to the Credit Card Companies
Failure to make an accepted Risk Weighted Calculation on Client Credit Cards - **Unreasonable** & **Exploitative**

Company	Rate	Period
BarclayCard x 2	26.5%	15 - 20 Years*
Capital One	34.0%	15 - 20 Years*
Marbles	39.9%	15 - 20 Years*
MBNA x 3	30.0%	15 - 20 Years*
Opus	48.1%	15 - 20 Years*
Royal Bank of Scotland	16.9%	15 - 20 Years*

Bank of England Base Rate – has been between 0.25% to 0.50%.
Client Repayment Record - **Excellent** to Perfect   Client CCE Creditworthiness - **AAA+**
*Each CreditCard will be able to confirm the exact **extortion period** and **interest rate** charged.
*The Financial Conduct Authority **(FCA)** have a watching brief but have failed **to date** to take action

(Centre inset: TimeOutCreditCards - The Story So Far No. 1 — Is long term bondage to credit card companies the scourge of our generation? Danny Moloney)

TimeOutCreditCards Collateralised Credit Exploitation: Extortion Index

---

@TimeOutCreditCards #PutAnEndToFinancialSlavery

Six Credit Cards Companies (NINE Cards) - the perpetrators are to be invited to meet the Financial Establishment - The Regulators at the 10 Downing Street Collateralised Credit Exploitation Summit 2018

TimeOutCreditCards Collateralised Credit Exploitation: PutAnEndToFinancialSlavery

TimeOutCreditCards Extortion Index

9 x Credit Cards from 6 Credit Card Companies Interest up to 48.1% (Bank Base Rate 0.25 to 0.50%)
Client Risk Weighted Asset – up to 1,151% positive return with NO Counter Party Risk to the Credit Card Companies
Failure to make an accepted Risk Weighted Calculation on Client Credit Cards – **Unreasonable & Exploitative**

TimeOutCreditCards - The Story So Far No. 1
Is long term bondage to credit card companies the scourge of our generation?
Danny Moloney

'Could or Should' the Credit Card Companies who have committed Collateralised Credit Exploitation be held to account for Persistent Mis - Representation ?

Bank of England Base Rate – has been between **0.25%** to **0.50%**
Client Repayment Record - **Excellent** to **Perfect**   Client **CCE** Creditworthiness - **AAA+**
*Each CreditCard will be able to confirm the exact **extortion period** and **interest rate** charged.
*The Financial Conduct Authority **(FCA)** have a watching brief but have **failed** to date to take action

TimeOutCreditCards Collateralised Credit Exploitation: Could or Should

Time Out Credit Cards
our Chancellors have failed the millions of vulnerable victims of Collateralised Credit Exploitation

UK citizens (perhaps up to 8,000 per constituency) have suffered long term debilitation and untold personal harm at the hands of Credit Card Companies perpetrating

Collateralised Credit Exploitation

| Capital One, Barclaycard & MBNA have capitalised on the financial slavery of Collateralised Credit Exploitation | Our Political - Financial - Regulatory Nexus have failed to protect vulnerable UK consumers. | RBS, New Day - Opus & Marbles have capitalised on the financial slavery of Collateralised Credit Exploitation |

TimeOutCreditCards Collateralised Credit Exploitation: Our Chancellors have FAILED!!!

HomiGenesis Signature

Covering the birth, nurturing and early growth of the unique

'Homigenesis - An Uniquely Individual Male Perspective' philosophy

Encompassing and developing the following key concepts;

Individual - Empathic - Gregarious - Thoughtful - Appreciative – Holistic

Presented & promoted via a combination of 1) academic research papers and specially created business, 2) Case studies, popular published **3)** e-books & 4) p-books, 5) formal lectures, 6) informative seminars, 7) Knowledge exchange presentations, 8) keynote speeches and 9) consultancy & 10) coaching.

Hashtags

#Homigenesis,

#ecclesiast, #hominist, #individuateur, #PrintMediateur, #TechnoPreneur #Originateur,

Research Formats

Insights - Spotlights - Signposts - Pathways - Foresights - Scenarios – Opportunities

Jaeger (1,000)   Chronologs (2,000)   **Genesis (5,000)**
Essays (10,000)   Stories (20,000)   Novels & Theses (80,000)

Each containing a uniquely innovative 'Homigenesis Moment' for
Ecclesiast - Hominist - Individuateur - Originateur - PrintMediateur - TechnoPreneur

See also and keep in touch on

Ecclesiast
Acquiring & Developing Knowledge via Community - Culture - Creativity - EnterPrise.

Hominist
: Acquiring & Developing Knowledge via Masculinity - Man - Male - Manly - Manliness.

Individuateur
Acquiring & Developing Knowledge via Data - Information - Analysis - Knowledge.

Originateur
Acquiring & Developing Knowledge via Originality - Lifelong Learning - Transculturation – Innovation

PrintMediateur
Acquiring & Developing Knowledge via Channel - Media - Marketing - Print.

TechnoPreneur
Acquiring & Developing Knowledge via Capacity - Capability - Competence - Opportunity.

Sunday 22nd July 2018

Thank you for reading

Billions will be Repaid to Millions - TimeOutCreditCards - Chris Wood

"""It should be easier for consumers to challenge unfair agreements and that the definition of 'extortionate' should be widened to cover unfair practices both at the time of entering the credit agreement as well as any subsequent events that may have led to unfairness""".

Part of GlobalMeHPTE, Greater Eccles, Manchester, United Kingdom.

Homigenesis

TechnoPreneur - Originateur - Hominist - Ecclesiast - Individuateur - Originateur

Tele: +44 7770 762860   Fax: + 44 161 789 8787

E-Mail: timeoutcreditcards@globalmehpte.com,

Words 5,009   **Images** - 24   **Pages** - 32

TimeOutCreditCards Collateralised Credit Exploitation – The Financial Scandal of our Generation

Financial Slavery by Credit Card Companies

No financial organization has the right to make excessive interest & charges on nominal amounts that cannot be paid back within an individual's lifetime.

Find Out More On: @TimeOutCCards and/or @DisCreditCards *and/or* TimeOutCreditCards – The Story So Far - No.1 https://www.amazon.co.uk/dp/B01N393PDI *and/or* What The FCA Should Know About Credit Cards https://www.amazon.co.uk/dp/B073Z1YVNT and/or Chronolog 'Talk To Us, Prime Minister' https://www.amazon.co.uk/dp/B07FC2TJHY and/or Chronolog 'Financial Slavery by Credit Card Companies' https://www.amazon.co.uk/dp/B07FM664XV and/or Genesis 'Billions will be REPAID to Millions – TimeOutCreditCards – Chris Wood

TimeOutCreditCards Collateralised Credit Exploitation: Never in the Annals of Financial History

www.ingramcontent.com/pod-product-compliance
Lightning Source LLC
Chambersburg PA
CBHW040343220526
45473CB00009B/2771